Trumping the Right Fantastic: Part 1

By Jeffrey L. Kelley

Dedication

This book is dedicated to my wife, Gabriela Kelley. If not for her continued encouragement and tender touch, I would not have finished this book before the end of the 2016 Presidential Election. I love her so much.

Heartfelt Thanks

I so appreciate the sacrifice of our, Gabriela and my, three boys - Charles, Gabriel, and Thomas. Our brief visits together, as I kept myself sequestered in a small room apart from their loving company, kept me motivated to push on toward my goal and deliver this manuscript on time.

Additional thanks goes out to Aunt Luci Alvarez de Diaz for listening to me ramble on in my best Castilian Spanish, and taking a deep and sincere interest in a political campaign within a country far and apart from her native country of Peru.

I would be remiss not to mention my son, Jeff Kelley, Jr, and my daughters, Rebecca Kelley Terry, and Mindy Kelley Van Pelt. They have been my source of inspiration for decades. I love you guys. You know it.

My in-laws provided a Peruvian touch to how U.S. Elections impact families of immigrants living in North America. Juan Celi Diaz voiced concern about his brother who lives on the west coast. Anahy Celi Diaz helped greatly with providing needed office functions, that would otherwise have taken me away from my keyboard.

Last, but not least, my sister Jean Kelley advised and inspired me to focus on printing my first volume as a digital download, as she had already done with her book, "As Friendly as a Thistle Weed" – on sale at Amazon Books. The distance from my friends and family in the States would have made it much more difficult to find a publisher willing to invest in a public sales campaign for my first volume. Thanks, sis!

There were many more people who encouraged, and inspired me to continue this emotional, stressful, and complicated work that, I hope, scratches below the surface of Donald J. Trump's quest to Make America Great Again. Thank you all for your cherished support.

Table of Contents

Preface

The title I chose for this book is a redefinition of the once popular phrase, "Trip the light fantastic." The original meaning meant 'to dance in a provocative or fantastic manner'. This saying was popular with the disco (discotheque) music and dance moves of the 1970's. Dance halls during the time were complemented by colorful flashing lights bouncing off mirrored globes. It was also the era when Donald Trump made his debut as a millionaire Manhattan real estate developer. One might imagine that 'The Donald' is a contestant in a dance contest, similar to those seen on the 1977 classic dance movie, 'Saturday Night Fever'. After a brutal combination of dance moves between various contestants, competitors were removed by roving judges one by one until only one person or couple remained on the dance floor. With this analogy in mind, 'Trumping the Right Fantastic' serves to demonstrate how Mr. Trump 'danced' or engaged his Conservative Right competitors one by one until he dominated them in a fantastic fashion.

Donald defeated the established politicians of the Republican Party by becoming the 'People's Choice' of the Republican Presidential Candidates. The Grand Old Party

(GOP) was shocked to realize that a real-estate mogul and Reality TV Star had overcome their 'rigged' political system to become the Republican Nominee for President of the United States. Many so-called Republicans have refused to accept him as his or her candidate, and have even gone so far as to vote for the Democratic Presidential Nominee, Hillary Rodham Clinton (HRC). This caused a split in the Republican National Convention (RNC), and has made it more difficult for Mr. Trump to secure votes during the General Presidential Election.

From early childhood, I have enjoyed playing with names and words. It has been more of a memory tool for me than of a tool to belittle others. Donald Trump's ability to associate social and heady mannerisms with the names of his competitors is something that has charmed me from the beginning. It often is seen as a juvenile political tactic. However, politics is seldom a mature and civil affair.

Most of us have experienced some amount of name-calling during our childhood. It is amazing how The Donald so effectively chided and humiliated the persona of the majority of his competitors. He, and I, learned first-hand that the verbal flagellation delivered by military drill instructors helps develop the intestinal fortitude needed to endure the rigors of intense competition. Mr. Trump's overpowering sureness, and the emotional insecurity of his competition proved too much for the other candidates. In the end, he received the confidence of over 15 million voters. It was the greatest victory in Republican Primary history.

No other candidate during this 2016 Presidential Campaign has the wealth of economic knowledge possessed by Mr. Trump. Standing on stage alongside his Republican counterparts during the Republican Presidential Primary Debates, he grated the nerves of several established politicians by reminding them, and the audience, of his past contributions to his or her past political campaigns. This was also a reminder to his audience that Mr. Trump had great political influence. One does not become a billionaire businessperson without rubbing elbows with powerful politicians.

Donald always speaks with authority. He doesn't back down, which is also one of his weaknesses. It's true that 'The Donald' has wasted time and energy on issues, which either should have been ignored, or turned to his advantage. Heroes aren't perfect. To the contrary, it is a hero's kryptonite that fills his admirers with hope that they too can achieve greatness.

A leader must demonstrate a humility that comes from his or her attachment with reality. Many times Donald Trump has stood on stage and credited the American people for his great success. Liars make excuses for his or her actions, and blame his or her calamity upon other people. President Harry Truman had a sign on his White House desk that read, "The buck stops here."

We have experienced eight years of passing the buck (shifting the blame) on to other people. Since President Obama first took office in 2008, he blamed our slow economic recovery from the Great Recession on President George W. Bush. While the country still remained in economic turmoil in 2012, he claimed to need another four years to overcome the failed policies of his predecessor. It's more than time for a US President who will take responsibility for his or her actions.

Donald J. Trump has dominated the headlines since he rode down the escalator at Trump Tower with his wife Melania on June 16, 2015. The MSM outrage he has evoked by his brash conduct and remarks would have caused most politicians to bow out of the race. Yet, Donald J. Trump does not back down from a confrontation. During the first Republican Debate, Donald told Debate Moderator Megyn

Kelly that a big problem we have in America today is that there is too much political correctness, or PC. It is Trump's aversion to PC that has freed the hearts and minds of tens of millions of US Citizens to express their discontent with the current political system. The machinations of Donald J. Trump are found by millions of Americans to be among his most endearing personal traits.

Many political analysts insisted Mr. Trump needed to make drastic changes to his mannerism and speech if he were to survive the general election, as he did not appear presidential. During the General Presidential Election, he has demonstrated that he has a presidential persona while being interviewed, during debates, and even during his many stadium-packed rallies.

Mr. Trump was not adept at using a teleprompter when he first appeared before the public. What many people tend to forget is that Mr. Trump has never held a political office. He seldom has had to cater to a sensitive public that is unaccustomed to the assertiveness, which made him a billionaire real estate mogul, and reality star.

It has been difficult for Mr. Trump to find a campaign manager who compliments his domineering spirit. Yet, after a little trial and error, he finally encountered a kindred spirit in his latest and greatest campaign manager, Kellyanne Conway. With VP Candidate, Mike Pence, Kellyanne Conway, and a host of political and surrogate powerhouses at his side, he has lifted himself from the political ashes and risen even stronger than ever before.

Today, Mr. Trump has to overcome the obstacles of unfaithful Republicans, the biased mainstream media, the corrupt Democratic National Convention (DNC), and the Clinton Foundation led by Bill and Hillary Clinton. He is struggling against all odds to overcome his adversaries and provide a leadership unhampered by hefty donor sponsorship, and foreign alliances. If elected, Donald Trump will not have to repay donors in the form of political favors. He has funded most of his campaign with his own assets, but also has received millions of dollars from his devoted fans. Howbeit, what he needs most is a small donation from the American people he will represent. One vote per person is a small price to pay for a great investment in America's future.

What will become of our hero? Can he muster enough votes from Republicans, Independents, and dissatisfied Democrats to make it to the White House? If ever there was a proverbial cliffhanger, which held the freedom and prosperity of America in the balance, this is the one that will make or break America. Donald J. Trump and Mike Pence must be elected in 2016. Tens of millions of Trump supporters have invested their hearts and souls to this end.

Introduction

My book extols and celebrates the political movement initiated by Donald J. Trump to overcome the failed leadership of established Washington-elite politicians, return our nation to a government 'Of the people, by the people, and for the people' and thereby 'Make America Great Again'. Mr. Trump promises to put 'America First' over global interests. Donald Trump is the first U.S. Presidential Nominee in modern political history to overcome the rigged system of a major political party. His sincere wish as President of the United States is to empower all American Citizens once again to have a voice in our nation's government.

"... this nation, under God, shall have a new birth of freedom -- and that government of the people, by the people, for the people, shall not perish from the earth."
Abraham Lincoln's Gettysburg Address, November 19, 1863 (Bliss Copy)

I invite everyone, especially the undecided, to review the history and facts of the Trump/Pence campaign. I will make it clear throughout this book that there are two distinctly different factions clamoring for your vote. Consider not only that the Washington establishment is deeply entrenched in keeping their lucrative positions on Capitol Hill, but also that the MSM is run by Liberal owners. Time studies of political coverage prove that the MSM have kept the lid on any negative political coverage of Hillary Clinton, while begging for more dirt on Donald Trump. I humbly solicit the intelligent voter to watch Fox News, read or watch the Wall Street Journal, or take advantage of news organizations that endeavor to promote truth in broadcasting this election.

While composing this book, I spent many hours watching videos and reading news articles concerning the 2016 U.S. Presidential Election. I also spent hours reading and contributing to commentaries of news articles on the internet. I have included a few of my more vociferous interchanges toward the end of the book. I have also endeavored to be forthcoming about news articles that have altered or bolstered my perception of the state of the presidential race. I have included the name of the article, author, hyper-link for those who want to learn more about each topic.

Donald J. Trump - Before the 2016 Election

The Childhood Years of Donald Trump

One thing I learned before reaching my golden years is that one's upbringing significantly contributes to, yet does not limit the person whom we will become. Psychologists refer to society's role in human development as the cultural influence of human growth and development. I am one who believes we are not limited by a modest childhood. On the other hand, if one is born in the right family under above-average circumstances, he or she has a greater chance of success in whatever endeavor he or she attempts to pursue. We have all witnessed someone who received that extra boost regardless of his or her education or talent. Nevertheless, Donald didn't need such pampering.

Donald John Trump was born on June 14, 1946, in Queens, New York, to a wealthy builder and real estate developer, and his wife - Frederick (Fred) C. and Mary MacLeod Trump. Fred Trump became wealthy during World War II by building apartments to accommodate the U.S. Navy workers who labored at major shipyards along the East Coast. His business experienced greater growth around

Coney Island and other locations around New York City. Donald was only a child at the time.

Donald J. Trump was a silver-spooner. Still, growing up and spending time with his father around construction sites gave him an appreciation for the men and women he encountered as the son of Fred Trump. Donald learned the business from the ground up. He was a fast learner, and enjoyed hanging out with the work crews, and managers of large housing projects. Yet, there was something in his persona, which required a higher sense of discipline and direction.

Donald was born the fourth of five children. Though, he was one of the brightest and most difficult to control. He had a lot of unbridled energy that needed to be harnessed in a disciplined fashion. His father decided the New York Military Academy was a good place to send young Donald, if he ever hoped to keep him out of serious trouble, and prepare him for a bright future in an increasingly competitive world. Academy life turned out to be fertile ground for young Donald Trump. He became captain of the Academy's baseball team, and graduated as a Captain, the NYMA's highest military rank.

Already, people knew that Donald Trump was an extraordinary person. He was born into money, but his energy and talent demonstrated he was destined to become a successful man by his own merit. He had a way with people, and would not settle for second best among his peers. Donald's natural and learned abilities, in addition to his father's connections in high society, would later propel him into coveted institutions of higher learning.

Influence is a two-edged sword in today's society. On one hand, we are expected to demonstrate a love for social networking, and teamwork in addition to improving our education and experience. On the other hand, some people are promoted above others simply because they have friends and family in high places. When we surrender good morals, and fair play to gain a public office, there is no turning back.

Having served over 20 years of military service, I can appreciate Donald Trump's experience in a military academy. Many critics point to the fact that Donald Trump never served in active or reserve military service. Our military services respect the training received by recruits who were reared and educated in a military school. They often receive advanced rank, service years, and commendations for their service. In

my opinion, Donald Trump experienced the rudimentary
values of military service.

Donald as a Young Adult

Donald continued to work with his father during summer vacations. He finally he decided to go into real estate with his father. Fred (Freddy) Trump, Jr., the elder heir of his father's business, had decided to become an airline pilot instead of continuing with real estate development. However, it was in Donald's blood to excel in business and become an heir to the Elizabeth Trump and Sons, Company. His first two years of college were invested in Fordham University in the Bronx, New York. However, after two years he found that he needed a greater challenge in education. Donald was accepted into the prestigious Wharton School of Finance at the University of Pennsylvania and graduated with a Bachelor's degree in Economics. His father hired him the same year, 1968, to work at Trump Management Company. In 1974, after only six years at Trump Management, Donald became president of the company.

Even before becoming the top executive at his father's firm, Mr. Trump had his eye on the highly lucrative Manhattan real estate across the East River. Fred advised Donald against investing in Manhattan, howbeit Donald persisted and finally won his father's blessing plus a cool one million dollar loan in seed money. Running a business apart from his father gave Donald the break he needed to prove himself in the real estate and construction business. Of course, he could always count on his father's influence (and millions of dollars) when making deals with city officials and influential business partners.

By the mid-1970s, Donald Trump was already worth over $200 million. He was described by Judy Klemesrud of the New York Times on November 1, 1976:

> "He is tall, lean and blond, with dazzling white teeth, and he looks ever so much like Robert Redford. He rides around town in a chauffeured silver Cadillac with his initials, DJT, on the plates. He dates slinky fashion models, belongs to the most elegant clubs and, at only 30 years of age, estimates that he is worth 'more than $200 million.' "

Donald Trump became one of the most famous citizens of New York City, and was credited for helping the city pull out of the fiscal slump it was in during the 1970–80s.

Mr. Trump, the Real Estate Mogul

One of Donald Trump's greatest strengths is his ability to use the reputation and money of others to accomplish his personal goals. It did not take long for people to discover that those who invested in Donald Trump made out big, including (as mentioned) the City of New York. By the time Donald had reached his thirties, he was extremely wealthy, popular, and one of Manhattan's most eligible bachelors. It was then that Donald Trump took the first step toward settling down from his playboy lifestyle. Today, Donald Trump continues his legacy as a real estate developer in other parts of the globe. Some of his projects are mentioned when discussing his first wife, Ivana.

Donald Trump the Author

The most popular book written by Donald J. Trump was 'The Art of the Deal', Published in 1987. Unnamed sources say over a million copies of the book were sold. During this 2016 Presidential Campaign, Donald boasted that it is "the number one selling business book of all time. In it, Mr. Trump gives advice on winning business strategies. There is also plenty of biographical information about the real estate magnate.

After a number of books on business, Donald Trump wrote a book titled, "The America we Deserve." Published in 2000, it is a notable book on public policy, and worth a read. Donald wrote the book early in his first attempt at running for President. In 2012, he wrote, "Time to Get Tough," within which he delivered a more Republican slant to his view on taxing the wealthy.

Donald Trump's most recent book is titled, "Crippled America: How to make America Great Again." It was later published under the title, "Great Again: How to fix our crippled America." In it, 'The Donald' voices his greatest concern, "In this book (previously published as Crippled America), we're going to look at the state of the world right now. It's a terrible mess, and that's putting it mildly. There has never been a more dangerous time. The politicians and special interests in Washington, DC are directly responsible for the mess we are in. So why should we continue listening to them?"

Donald Trump has authored over a dozen books both political and business in nature, which have earned him millions of dollars. Yet, one rarely becomes a billionaire solely by writing books. He has appeared for numerous television interviews and appeared on Time Magazine numerous times, especially during his campaign for President. Writing and publicity has been in his blood for decades. Today, his prodigious efforts in commerce, real estate development, and negotiations with corporations, both foreign and domestic, has honed his leadership skills to profound levels of acuity.

Donald Trump the Reality Television Star

It is difficult for me to imagine how anyone can have the time and energy to run a multi-billion dollar enterprise, write books, and star in a television series simultaneously. Nevertheless, Donald Trump accomplished this and more. In addition, he has a lovely, intelligent, and successful family. Donald's television series, The Apprentice, and Celebrity Apprentice drew a dedicated and massive following. Mr. Trump could have continued his series, but refused to sign another contract. Why? We all know that his desire to become President of the United States far outweighs other more lucrative pursuits.

The Apprentice series pitted a group of business want-to-be's in a contest to see if he or she had what it takes to be an executive in The Trump Organization. The prize, "You're hired." It was the ultimate job interview. Of course, Donald Trump's most famous phrase was, "You're fired." Imagine the blow to one's ego to be fired on television. Nevertheless, many of those 'losers' went on to become successful due to his or her notoriety. A number of them even returned to compete in the Celebrity Apprentice. As Donald nears the end of this grueling race for President, one can see that his opponent does not have the energy to make the campaign trail a campaign superhighway like Donald. I cannot imagine many people could. Donald Trump has the advantage with public opinion. He has been an unconquerable public figure since the day he 'took' Manhattan. Frank Sinatra's lyrics, "I'll take Manhattan," within his legendary song 'Manhattan' adequately describes Donald J. Trump's claim to fame.

Donald's First Wife – Ivana Zelnickova

Ivana Marie Zelnickova was living in New York while promoting the 1976 Montreal Olympics. Ivana was born in Czechoslovakia, and her father helped her develop her natural talent for skiing. She went to a language school in Canada to become more fluent in English. Ivana had already been married once before to real estate agent Alfred Winklmayr from 1971 to 1973. In addition to her years as a professional skier, she modeled furs in Canada. Ivana must have made an impression on the New York elite, as it was unlikely she could have bumped into Donald at a local nightclub, as Donald Trump does not drink alcohol, smoke, or do drugs. Nevertheless, their public appearances left an impression on New Yorkers, and they decide to marry. On April 7, 1977, Donald and Ivan married and became the darling couple of Manhattan.

Ivana proved to be a remarkable businessperson and designer. She worked with Donald on several building projects, including the renovation of the Grand Hyatt Hotel, the Trump Taj Mahal Casino Resort in Atlantic City, New Jersey, and Trump Tower on Fifth Avenue in Manhattan, New

York. Ivana is credited for making Trump Tower one of the most fashionable buildings in Manhattan.

Donald and Ivana had three children together. Donald John Trump Jr. was born December 31, 1977 in Manhattan, New York. It was nearly four years later when Ivanka Marie Trump was born on October 30, 1981. The youngest of their children, Eric Frederick Trump, was born just over two years later on January 6, 1984. Although they tried to shield the children the best they could, the high-profile divorce of Donald and Ivana in 1992 was heartbreaking. Ivana initiated the divorce due to Donald's love affair with model Marla Maples. The two had put business first before family, and drifted apart. Yet, it was Donald who began to crave his old life as a Manhattan playboy.

Donald's Second Wife - Marla Maples

Sometimes, the other woman reaps a reward for her indiscretion. Marla became 'the other woman' in 1989. Ivana gave Donald a lot of space before she filed for divorce in 1991. Evidently, Donald's relationship with Marla was one of convenience, at first. However, more than a year after his divorce with Ivana, he married Marla in December of 1993 at New York's Plaza Hotel. Marla was born on October 27, 1963, and more than 17 years younger than Donald. Howbeit, she was already nearly thirty years old as Donald neared fifty. Could Donald make it work this time? When Tiffany Ariana Trump was born October 13, 1993, it seemed as if they were in it for the long haul. However, Donald's second marriage only lasted six years this time around. In 1999, when Tiffany was only six years old, Donald and Marla parted matrimonial ways.

Donald's Third Wife - Melanija (Melania) Knavs

Melanija Knavs, later to become Melania Knauss, was born in Novo Mesto, Slovenia, Yugoslavia on April 26, 1970. Melania speaks five languages, and is a former model. She became a permanent resident of the U.S. in 2001 and a citizen in 2006. In 1998, before Donald Trump's divorce with Marla was final, Melania and Donald met at a Fashion Week party in New York City. Melania was reluctant to date Donald, at first and even broke off her relationship with him for a few months. They eventually reconciled and maintained an extended relationship. It wasn't until 2004 before they became engaged, and then married on January 22, 2005.

On March 20, 2006, Baron William Trump was born to Donald and Melania. He is now over ten years old as his father, Donald J. Trump, nears the end of a brutal Presidential Campaign. If Donald Trump should win the election, he and his mother Melania will join Donald at their new residence, 1600 Pennsylvania Avenue, Washington, D.C.

Disclaimer

I felt it prudent to keep many of the details of Donald J. Trump's years before his presidential candidacy brief in order to focus on his current campaign. Time is running short, and this book is dedicated to a general overview of his race for President of the United States. With enough reader interest, my next book, Trumping the Right Fantastic: Part 2, will cover more details of the General Election, and what helped him win (or lose) the election.

Donald J. Trump the Presidential Candidate

The Announcement

I can still picture Melania and Donald Trump gliding down the escalator within Trump Tower in New York City. A few steps away a boatload of reporters were waiting for his announcement for his candidacy for President of the United States. I was not fortunate enough to witness this historic event in person. My home is now in Chiclayo, Peru. My main connection to my beloved country, the United States of America, is via the internet and television. I watched him make his announcement later on the internet, and heard him say, "Ladies and Gentlemen, I am officially running for President of the United States, and we are going to make our country great again."

Finally, I thought, there is someone who really understands the desires and needs of the silent majority. It seemed like most of our country was in denial. The Liberal media had helped the Obama/Clinton administration lull America to sleep. Donald Trump's announcement was a call to arms for many people who wanted real change, not the fabricated change of President Barack Obama. Millions of people who respected and followed Donald Trump over the years began to pledge his or her support to our fledgling candidate for President. His rallies were more packed than most sporting events, or rock concerts. Most often, many attendees had to wait outside and listen to his speeches from loudspeakers. Fans arrive early, and long lines always accompany his events. This was the beginning of hope for many jobless Americans. Donald Trump is the rejuvenated voice of the silent majority.

What Donald Trump has to Offer

'The Donald' is a shrewd negotiator; he and his top executives have negotiated with many corporations and a number of nations, and have won the better part of the deal. Mr. Trump often speaks about winning at his rallies. "We don't win anymore," he announces. Nonetheless, he offers solutions to our many economic, international trade, and political woes. Our political representatives have driven us into debt, while providing economic prosperity to our global competitors, such as China, Japan, Mexico, and Vietnam. We purchase products free of import taxes, and ship our jobs overseas. They, on the other hand, impose import taxes on our exports or reject them outright. The half- trillion-dollar trade imbalance with China demonstrates how the Obama Administration has sold us down the Yangtze River.

Why is Donald Trump Running for President?

Imagine you are a successful businessperson, and maybe you are. You have made your fortune, and have hired the right people to run your business. Now, you have the opportunity to retire and enjoy the fruits of your labor. You consider visiting countries and cultures you have always wanted to experience and explore. Maybe, you could start or enlarge a charity, and become an integral part of helping thousands of people.

On the other hand, you could be President of the United States. Wait a minute; isn't that position reserved for those who have spent decades in politics, or in courts of law, or even the military? How many successful people wait until retirement age to take on the rigors of the highest office in the land? We know one in this day and age who has committed himself to at least four years of the grueling work of heading the greatest nation on Earth – Donald J. Trump.

Well, just because you are wealthy, popular, intelligent, resourceful, and successful doesn't necessarily qualify you for the office of POTUS. You could be someone much less competent. Recent political history has proven that to be true. In my naïve younger years as a citizen of the United States, I had wondered why there were so few truly successful people who cared to run for president. In my imagination I thought, maybe it just doesn't pay enough for the wealthy to spend their valuable time when other capable people were willing to sacrifice a few years of privacy to gain power and prestige. Certainly, those who have been President have been in great demand and can make millions in book sales and speaking fees. I believe our Commander in Chief loses a few years of longevity in this office of high stress, long hours, and relentless publicity.

Considering the latter, who would want to give up a life of comfort and luxury to place himself or herself in harm's way? Is the glory and power so alluring that it is worth all the effort, or is there something else at play? Donald J. Trump has already stated that our country has fallen in great disrepair. Many citizens are living in poverty, and many have just decided to quit the workforce. Donald believes he can restore America to its former glory. Who are we to turn away someone who wants to give back to a country who enabled him to become successful and wealthy? We all know that Hillary Clinton wants prestige and power. I think of the day when each of them lies upon his and her deathbed and considers what

Clinton Debacles

What Ails Hillary

Saturday, September 03, 2016

What ails Hillary Clinton? I mean, what really AILS Hillary? We may discover her affliction(s) on September 26, 2016 when she debates Donald Trump on stage in front of millions upon millions of people worldwide. Is that what we want the world to see as a Democratic Candidate for President of the United States? Whatever truth can be ascertained from the media is quickly squelched by the Liberal hounds seeking to keep the truth of her wellness well up the tree and out of public sight.

Hillary Clinton has had no press conference for nine months – <u>nine months</u>! What is that all about? Does she think Donald Trump will go easy on her any more so than the sixteen professional politicians he walloped during the Presidential Primaries? Has she prepared every excuse for every time she plays 'Frozen Angel', goes bonkers like she has several times in full public view, or her inability to stand without the aid of the Secret Service? She stated she had fully recovered from a blood clot she had suffered while taking a 'spill' in 2012. Yet, years later, she told the FBI she doesn't recall much after suffering from a blood clot in 2012. Will she use the same excuse for making bad decisions during her hopeful presidency?

The American public deserves to know what type of physical impairment Hillary has before it is too late. Are Democrats really voting for Tim Kaine for president? After all, he is next in succession. Will all the millions of dollars she is amassing from wealthy donors go toward a Kaine campaign? Maybe, we should have Kaine debate Trump. As far as we know, he is much healthier than Hillary. The only thing that keeps the hounds at bay is the Liberal press, and even that is beginning to fade. As it stands, Hillary has kept the door open for President by placing her foot in the doorjamb to keep it from slamming shut. However, after a few healthy door slams by Donald Trump, even that will no longer be an option.

legacy they have left behind. Which would you want, the adoration and appreciation of millions of people around the world, or the glory of being the first in your race, sex, or faith to obtain the office of President of the United States? Glory fades, yet adoration endures. The most popular Presidents are those who do their best to help the world and not to help his or her own selfish ambitions.

The Trump Family

As mentioned earlier, Donald Trump has a total of five children from three separate marriages. The three oldest, Don Jr., Ivanka, and Eric Trump work as Vice-Presidents for the Trump Organization. Their younger sister, Tiffany Trump, just graduated from college, and reportedly is seeking employment. She is hoping to reconnect with her father after living in California for years. Baron Trump, the youngest, may be the only Trump child to live in the White House with his mother, Melania, and President Trump.

If Donald Trump becomes President, the three older Trumps will be in charge of Trump Organization. A recent interview with the siblings seems to indicate that Ivanka may become its president. We will soon find out how things will shake out after November 8. Donald plans to put all his energy into Making America Great Again. His business prowess is sure to translate to a booming economy for the United States, and his 'America First' policies will equate to hundreds of thousands of new jobs. Melania will have a new job as an active first lady. Move over, Jackie Kennedy.

The Main Stream Media and Mr. Trump

USA Article

"This year, the choice isn't between two capable major party nominees who happen to have significant ideological differences. This year one of the candidates – Republican nominee Donald Trump – is, by unanimous consensus of the Editorial Board, unfit for the presidency.

From the day he declared his candidacy 15 months ago through this week's first presidential debate, Trump has demonstrated repeatedly that he lacks the temperament, knowledge, steadiness, and honesty that America needs from its presidents." *USA Today Editorial Board*

Commentary of USA Article

You know, most of us do not have to do a lick of research to understand how liberally slanted, and moronic the opinion of these so-called Editors appear to the public. I wonder what the undecided independent voters think about this piece of garbage. Okay, here is my unapologetic and snarky reply.

"Oh, I get it. We need a president that either screams at reporters, or bores small crowds to oblivion. The next President must be a woman who receives donations from foreign governments, and supports governments who: do not permit women to drive, make them cover themselves from head to foot, keep them at home unless they have a male escort, keep them out of college or work without the permission of a male, and subject them to death by stoning for any suspicion of nonconformity.

Mrs. President must be someone who does not remember the years she served as Secretary of State, when testifying to the FBI. She must be someone who needs constant rest and medical care after multiple falls and blackouts. Finally, she must be someone who lies to the public, the FBI, and Congress. Thanks for clearing that up for me. Hey, USA Today, since you know more than tens of millions of Republicans, I guess your articles are just too difficult for us to understand. Goodbye and good riddance." Former Readers of USA Today, The Kelley's of Peru

Commentary

The Liberal media and polling agencies would have Trump fans believe our hero is failing. Great generals use such strategies to draw their enemy into battle. Early in the General Election, Hillary was playing hide and seek with hopes all her crooked deeds will magically fade away. For her, no news about her is good news.

From my perspective, Fox News has been our greatest media ally. They have provided unbiased journalism, which is why Hillary Clinton and her surrogates have avoided interviews with reporters from Fox News. Trump Rallies have provided spectacular events that have lured the biased media networks, such as CNN, CBS, NBC, and others into giving the news-starved public brief peeks into the popularity of Donald Trump. During the Presidential Primary Elections, Mr. Trump had coaxed the Liberal media into covering his winning messages by making off-the-cuff-comments, which caused them to go into a 'feeding frenzy' of negative journalism. Our candidate has used whatever he could to get attention with the hope that a few of his positive messages would eke out into the general public.

I found it entertaining to watch Mr. Trump and Governor Cruz duke it out with Governor Kasich tied to the bumper like a bouncing tin can on a honeymooner's automobile. Except for Ohio, he was always a part of the cleanup crew. He was a laughing hyena waiting for the scraps left over from a Lion's kill. "Why should I get out of the race?" In a mental state of confusion, he must have thought this motto would get him selected at the Republic National Convention. Even after Kasich decided to drop out of the race, he continues to pout. When the RNC held its Primary Election Nomination in Cleveland, Ohio. this poor hapless Governor didn't even appear to welcome the RNC into his state. After millions of dollars were pouring into Buckeye coffers, this sad sack blustered on his tracks like an 'Engine that (never) could'.

Trump Debacles

Donald Trump Does Not Always Thrill

Monday, June 06, 2016

This is my opportunity to come clean about some of the misgivings I have with my favorite Presidential Candidate, Donald Trump. The recent lawsuit against the belated Trump University has made me uncomfortable with Mr. Trump's decision-making skills. Even people I respect from Fox News have questioned his penchant for controversy and unbending urges to attack anyone he feels is out to get him. Can he control his anxiety to 'counterpunch' at every wisp of impropriety?

Mr. Trump has many admirable qualities. Yet, as our future President, he cannot go off half-cocked and become a menace to his own shadow. I know that he feels he is not getting a fair deal with the current judge in the lawsuit against him. However, publicly attempting to force the Hispanic judge off the case may not be the best way to handle the situation.

However, I pause to mentally review what occurs during a jury trial. The jurors are chosen according to gender, race, ethnicity, age, et. al. Are judges also examined under the same criteria? Still, we must follow procedure. Attorneys representing Trump can "petition the administrative judge in that district for a remedy" or "file to remove the venue from the judge," says Newt Gingrich. However, Mr. Trump must be willing to accept the new judge and not play a game of revolving doors. A judge is not that same as a jury member. Judges are held to higher standards, and elected by the people because of his or her high standards. A jury is not so clearly vetted. Attorneys for the plaintiff and defense hope to have the majority of jurors who may be more sympathetic to his or her cause. Whereas, a judge must be sympathetic to no one.

Most people, especially Trump supporters (such as I), believe most of what Donald Trump has done has raised the bar for equal treatment of the middle class, as well as minorities. The American majority has been left gasping for air by the Obama Administration. We are not treated fairly by the Liberal press. Our rights and security have been replaced by an overzealous and unreasonable concern for minority groups. The prime taxpayers of America have seen their quality of life diminish as illegal immigrants receive a free ride. I firmly believe that if an illegal immigrant or a minority had complained about a 'white' judge there would be no discussion and the judge would be replaced by one sympathetic to his or her cause.

Here is something else to consider. Maybe, Donald Trump is showing the American majority how he or she can fight back against bigotry from minorities. The typical Euro-American has been marginalized by the minorities. What has happened is that many minorities feel they are the only ones who can play the 'race' card. We have been told that we have 'white privilege'. In other words, anyone who does not fit within one's minority group is automatically a bigot. We all have a race, and we all have to consider if we are getting equal treatment. If this is the point that Mr. Trump is trying to make, rather than simply personal gain, he should state it clearly. It is his openness and plainness of speech that has rewarded him the ear of most Americans. We need to hear a better explanation from him so we are better able to explain it to those who may be considering voting for the opposition.

The Down Ballot - Buy the Numbers (not a misspelling)

- <u>Democrats</u> will have to gain five (5) seats from the Republicans to take the majority of the Senate. They have 10 seats up for reelection, which means they <u>Need To Win 15 Seats</u>.

- <u>Republicans</u> have 24 seats up for reelection. They <u>Need To Win 20 Seats</u>.

This appears to put Republicans at a disadvantage except when one considers that Republicans, in order to keep the majority, only need to <u>maintain</u> 20 or their 24 seats up for reelection. Any wins of Democrat seats by Republicans is icing on the cake. Remember, an incumbent Senator (on average) has the greater advantage during an election. Even if the Democrats kept all their seats, unlikely as it may be, they would have to unseat at least five (5) Republicans to take over the Senate.

However, let's be honest and consider that the Democrats could lose a couple seats. Now, they have to unseat seven (7) Republicans. Each seat that the Democrats lose means one more they have to gain from the Republicans.

The incumbent advantage actually gives Republican Senators and edge to keep their majority standing.

Republican Presidential Primaries

When the second state, New Hampshire, came up for grabs there were only eight (Trump, Rubio, Kasich, Cruz, Bush, Christie, Fiorina, and Carson) of the original seventeen candidates left to compete for the Republican Presidential ticket. On February 9, 2016 only three candidates exceeded the expectations of pollsters: Trump, Kasich, and Christie. However, the top three slots went to Trump (35.3), Kasich (15.8), and Cruz (11.7). Could Kasich have won New Hampshire without Trump in the mix? It's questions like this that really come to mind when one considers comments by 'establishment' politicians that someone other than Donald Trump should have been the Nominee. Yet, Donald Trump had more than doubled the votes of his closest competitor, Governor Kasich. Furthermore, Kasich only beat out Cruz by 4 points. I must also mention that Rubio was behind Cruz by only about 1 point and Bush was less than 1 point behind. The other contestants were only chatter at this point, and disappeared almost as quickly.

PolitiSpeak

When a politician pretends to inform the public without delivering any tangible information, they are using a technique called PolitiSpeak. The dullest of all PolitiSpeak is when an elected official gives the same response, even when a question is phrased in a different manner. Senator Ted Cruz is an expert in this regard. He does not flinch, or show any telltale remorse for answering questions in such a misleading fashion. Donald Trump called him Lyin' Ted for just such a reason. Fabrication of false information or distorting the truth is what journalism is made of these days.

Anyone familiar with business negotiations knows that an first offer is always more than what a negotiator needs or even expects. He or she understands there must be some give and take in the process. This is what Donald J. Trump announces to the public. It is his best offer for any project or campaign promise he promotes. Of course, this sounds outlandish to most people. Yet, this is the norm for the business world.

This is the world we live in today. International trade should never be a one-way proposition. When U.S. politicians (people who are mostly unfamiliar with the business world) make an offer, they make a 'reasonable' proposition. When this happens, the United States has already lost the negotiation. In addition, countries such as Iran need an extra dose of fantasy propositions. We should expect outrage from grandiose offers. Yet, as long as there is room for compromise, nobody should walk away from the table. Those who walk away must only do so from a position of strength. The opponent must be willing to offer something new to entice further negotiations.

The news media looks for every opportunity to land a story. Most news organizations lean toward the left. That is because their readership is the most gullible, and the owners support the politicians who do their bidding. However, some correspondents and writers are not as astute as the people they wish to 'expose'. Sometimes, it is difficult to separate ignorance from deception. If a reporter is anxious to please his boss, he or she may play dumb. Either way, whether for play, or in reality, this type of reporting is dishonest. This is why Donald Trump consistently points out the dishonestly of the news media.

This is what would happen if the news began to return to factual reporting. During Trump rallies, the public would be astounded by the crowds The Donald attracts. They would also laugh at Hillary Clinton rallies, and be more enthused by Bernie Sanders rallies. While television stations would get higher ratings, the owners and CEOs would get fewer kickbacks from political donors. What people need to understand is that competition and ratings are important to the livelihood of the media. Nevertheless, it is second to the profits of the owners. It is great if the owners can score a double-win, yet they often settle for more money in their own pockets.

What really scares the Republican and Democratic Parties about Donald Trump is that all the donations they have been receiving from corporations and special interest groups may soon go away. Could it be that the average American citizen may finally receive what he or she is worth? If Donald trump could return even a fraction of the money and power hoarded by the upper 10% of the earners in the United States, it would be a historical triumph for Middle America. We can only hope against all hope that those who really contribute to the success of American industry will receive his or her just due.

A Great Rival Bids Adieu

May 3. 2016

Elation is a great intoxicant. When we are flying high, it is difficult to focus on other events around us. The U.S.

Primary Presidential Election of 2016 is one of these intoxicating times. As Donald J. Trump captures the hearts of Hoosiers in Indiana, I find it challenging to take my attention off the internet and television. As I write this, Carly Fiorina is speaking on national television as Senator Ted Cruz is being defeated by double digits in one of our nation's Great Lake States. She spoke about how much she loves the campaign she serves and all the faithful contributors and voters that have supported the one whom they all had hoped would be the next President of the United States. It was evident that something was amiss. It was less than a week before when Presidential Candidate Cruz had asked her to become his VP running mate in a move that they and others had hoped would invigorate their dying campaign.

While Ms. Fiorina spoke, my wife showed me a bracelet she had created from ornate beads and silver figurines. I forced myself to direct my attention toward her lovely creation, while ignoring the historic event that was unfolding. My wife speaks little English, and has only kept up on this election through the brief Spanish conversations we had had, and the perfunctory news coverage she had seen on Peruvian television. My sons hear my whoops and hollers, and I occasionally hear my youngest mimicking my cheers and jeers of an event that had captivated my patriotic spirit.

Lyin' Ted, Corrupt Hillary, and Low-energy Jeb, these are all a few of the nicknames The Donald had so effectively associated with a few of his political foes. The politically correct press and public ridicule 'The Donald' for his infantile tactics. All the while, his barbs eat away at the thin platforms his adversaries had created. They ask themselves why their ruses no longer give them the edge they had enjoyed in past political endeavors. Do their years of success all boil down to kindergarten tactics of name calling, bullying, and skinned knees?

Donald Trump had once been associated with professional wrestling – the grownup version of neighborhood brawls. On the other hand, his years of notoriety on The Apprentice, and stellar success as real estate tycoon has touched many of the hearts and minds across America. Does showmanship trump statesmanship? Alternatively, do they both share a common thread within our DNA?

Popularity often outsmarts common sense during elections. Obama pats himself on the back for his reelection. All the while the intelligencia knows his political losses far outweigh his success as President. A sitting president has a huge home court advantage over most incumbents. Add to his popularity the significance of being the first 'black' president, and it becomes a difficult task to uproot him.

The ridicule of Donald J. Trump by the 'politically correct' has done little to assuage his giant following. Every Trump rally is attended by crowds of fans that exceed the capacity of the stadiums and concert halls his campaign had rented. No other candidate has drawn hundreds of protestors against his presidential run. Mr. Trump has accepted most all invitations for personal and phone interviews. Due to his overwhelming popularity, he has racked up billions of dollars in free advertising for his campaign. That is fortunate for him, as he is the only candidate who is self-funding.

The Donald Trump and Mike Pence Ticket

About Hillary Clinton

Hillary Rodham Clinton is President Barrack Hussein Obama's right-hand woman. Therefore, to elect Madame Hillary is to elect another 1461 days of an Obama nation. Let's consider a similarity between the two impeached presidents of the 20th century. President Nixon and President Clinton were both impeached by Congress. They both committed crimes unworthy of the Executive Branch of our government. President Barrack Obama has been operating from the Nixon/Clinton playbook. President Nixon once said, "I am not a crook." President Obama once said, "I am not a tyrant."

Hillary Clinton is the former first lady of the Clinton Presidency. She has inherited all the schemes, favoritism, and wealth of her husband and former President Bill Clinton. She used the popularity of her husband and her sex to gain office into the Senate. Later, she used the same attributes to become Secretary of State under President Barrack Obama. Mrs. Clinton has already stated that she will put her husband, president Bill Clinton, in charge of the economy. In other words, she has pre-abdicated a portion of her presumed future presidency to former President Clinton. If this should come to pass, it may be an illegal act, as President Clinton has already served two terms as President of the United States.

Because of her nefarious deeds while serving as First Lady, a Senator of New York, and Secretary of State, she has become a flawed candidate for the DNC. She has badgered her husband's lovers. She has used money from The Clinton Foundation, which in turn receives funds from countries who persecute gays, and dominate women. She failed to act during the attack on the US Embassy in Benghazi, and caused the death of its Ambassador, and three other people. She circumvented the security safeguards she swore to uphold while Secretary of State, and exposed highly classified information to foreign governments by placing Top Secret documents on her computer server at her personal residence. These and many other scandalous and traitorous deeds Mrs. Clinton has committed during her political career.

About Donald J. Trump

Presidential candidate Donald J trump has given her a nickname, Crooked Hillary. In one of his speeches, Mr. Trump stated that Hillary Clinton, if she were a man, would only receive 5% of the popular vote. A better title, then, for Ms. Clinton would be to call her Madam 5%. That is because most of her supporters want her to be president simply because she is a woman. This is similar to President Obama's candidacy as the first African American President.

Just as what we have seen with the passing of Brexit, Donald J Trump has foretold not only the transformation of the United States, but of the world. Britain has determined that their citizens have moved beyond the barbarisms of Third World Cultures, and they do not want to return to the Middle Age battles between Islam and Christianity. Britain and the US want to enjoy the prosperity that innovative thinking and winning cultural mannerisms have to offer. We will see more countries join our movement as the days and weeks progress. The Brexit Train and the Trump Train are heading down the tracks. Those who accept altruism and prosperity and reject barbarism and poverty are welcome to join us.

Overview of the Presidential Election Process

I thought it would be appropriate to add some information about our Presidential Election Process in the United States. As I researched the process, there were a few things that I had forgotten, or never knew. I hope you find this as enlightening as I have.

- Election of President of the United States occurs every four years on the first Tuesday after the first Monday in November. November 8 is election day in 2016.

Election Process of a Political Party Nominee

1. Primary elections and caucuses
2. Nominating Conventions – a nominee is selected
3. <u>Nominee announces a Vice Presidential running mate from a state other than his home state.</u>
4. Party candidate campaigns across the country
   - Explains views and plans to voters
   - Participates in debates with other party candidates

General Election

1. Popular Vote – Registered U.S. Citizens cast their vote at his or her designated polling station selected according to primary physical residence. Or, they may vote by absentee ballot sent to the city/county office within his or her voting district.
2. Electoral College

> A candidate must receive the majority of electoral votes.

> <u>If no candidate receives the majority, the House of Representatives chooses the President, and the Senate chooses the Vice President.</u>

Where it all Began

Any event as complex as a US Presidential election is a virtual collage of people and places. It is where, one has to believe, a whole lifetime could be spent deciphering all the details without even describing effectively what actually transpired. This is especially true when one of those persons happens to be Donald J. Trump. Mr. Trump is both a phenomenon and an enigma to political reporters, pundits, analysts, and so-called consultants who only listen to what The Donald has said while inferring the worst instead of grasping his intent.

Standing on the stage of his first Republican Candidate Debate, he informed everyone that he was not a believer in political correctness (PC). Nobody could really comprehend the full intent of his deliberation until the bodies of 'Watch what you say' began to pile up and cast a stink across

Washington, and the American public. Slowly, but surely, 'The Silent Majority' began to come out of his or her shell and began telling a tale that was held hostage in the hearts and minds of millions of American citizens. They knew they had a leader they could believe in. He was the voice of the politically oppressed. He was the Abraham Lincoln of the politically enslaved, and the Ronald Reagan of the economically disadvantaged. All classes of people, who were not ashamed to call Donald Trump their friend, could now unite under a common banner, "Make America Great Again."

Donald Trump's reign officially began in July 22, 2016 on a stage in Cleveland, Ohio, smack dab in the middle of America's Rust Belt. It was a meager, howbeit auspicious moment in which political chastity clashed with constitutional destiny. For, who could argue that the People's Candidate, billionaire Donald J. Trump, could not have been a more appropriate representative of those who make America great?

We can now focus on concepts and projects that unite all of us under a common banner. This land is our land, and it has borders. We are a country who is part of a fair and just global economy. We can no longer be the country that provides security for other free nations at a human and economic discount. Immigrants are welcome, if they enter America legally and agree to share in American values, laws, and democracy.

I was not a believer in Donald Trump in the beginning. I had spent years in retail sales observing, yet not appreciating, the brash tactics of salespeople who were out for the buck on those down on their luck. The Apprentice reminded me of those days, and how I despised the domineering spirit of people who knew how to spin silk out of cotton. Reality shows have never been my 'thing'. Consequently, when I first watched on the internet Mr. Trump glide down the escalator with his wife, Melania, providing a pleasant distraction, I was not nearly as impressed as I am, today.

Some people still cling to Mr. Trump's television persona, or focus on media slams about the huge bankruptcies during his rise to fame and fortune in New York, and New Jersey. The mainstream media (MSM) refuse to consider the 'big picture', as readers and viewers often prefer scandals and controversy over prosperity and success. Then, when you throw in one of America's well-known political figures, Hillary Clinton, it becomes obvious to the bottom-feeders of public opinion that Donald is a squatter on the political turf of the Washington elite.

The most entertaining part of Donald Trump's reputation, as the so-called leader of a 'carnival act' for the uneducated and vociferous crowd, is that he rankles the 'Establishment' politicians, which so many people despise. Mr. Trump's followers are primarily those who are tired of the hundreds of campaign promises delivered throughout the decades, which rarely come into fruition. Furthermore, America has become like a tired shopper who believes what every salesperson tells them, and forgets about what America needs. People claim that Donald Trump has no clue about politics, yet he wouldn't have made his billions without understanding what politicians want.

Big Issues

Crossing the Line

One of the most pleasurable theme a Trumpster will hear at a Trump rally is Donald Trump's stance on 'The Wall' - the proposed giant wall, which will run across the border between the United States and Mexico. Everyone knows the reason as to why we have so many illegal immigrants and drug traffickers in America is that our southern border security is easy to circumvent. Our first line of defense in controlling illegal entry into the United States is the fence-line or wall across our southern border. Eyewitness testimony and documentaries have attested to its vulnerability. Criminals have burrowed underneath the wall, built ramps to drive over the wall, and have entered the US through openings in the wall.

Furthermore, the Obama administration has often ordered that tens of thousands of illegal aliens, even known criminals, captured by border security are to be released by Border Patrol agents. He has allowed the creation of Sanctuary Cities where illegal immigrants can take shelter from Immigration Agents. Some criminals have been caught and released dozens of times. The high influx of minimum wage workers have cost many US Citizens their jobs. Businesses have illegally, hired illegal immigrant workers to improve their bottom line. Illegal immigration is a large contributor to our high unemployment rate in America.

America: Land of the free and home of the slave

We have a growing population of 'Undocumented Workers' in the US because immigrants know that our current Welfare State will care for them and their families using taxpayer dollars. Welfare recipients do not pay taxes, as their income falls below the poverty line in taxpayer income. In addition, they receive compensation for the number of people in their household. Welfare benefits are so easy to obtain, even for American workers, that many US Citizens refrain from reentering the workforce as their pay and benefits would decrease substantially. Unfortunately, men and women who 'voluntarily' stay at home soon lose his or her competitive edge in the workplace. Those workers who choose to return to the workforce are denied jobs based on their long-term unemployment history. These disenfranchised workers have become slaves of the State. The chances for these men and women of becoming self-sufficient citizens, and raising a happy and healthy family have been greatly diminished.

Disenfranchised Workers

Our government's definition of unemployment only encompasses active participants in unemployment benefits and those actively seeking employment. Once a worker ceases to meet the reporting criteria for unemployment, they are discounted by the Department of Labor. They have become disenfranchised from our nation's workforce. The number of disenfranchised workers is so large that our unemployment rate could possibly more than double with their inclusion. Donald Trump has pointed out on numerous occasions that our unemployment rate is not accurate. He rightfully asserts that President Obama has misled the public on lower unemployment rates. It's easy to see that the number of jobs added to the workforce cannot substantiate lower unemployment. Hundreds of thousands of new workers enter the workforce every year. High school and college graduates have to take part-time jobs or jobs well below their education level in order to gain a meager income. College graduates usually have large government-backed college loans to repay. Their repayment is based upon their ability to pay. In order words, our government has funded college education will less chance of repayment than ever before.

America First

Any good police detective knows that determining motive and proving it through evidence, is the most difficult part of an investigation. I am not a detective, yet (like everyone else) I have my own opinions concerning Donald J. Trump. Magicians are masters at using smoke and mirrors. Psychologists are good at diagnosing mental illness through mannerisms and symptoms. People like Donald Trump know what motivates people and what to do to earn their trust. He is a great negotiator. The things he says and does are all calculated based on risk and rewards.

The Donald also is an expert with the media. He is familiar with all forms of communication. Does he miscalculate on occasion? Sure he does. Yet, he rarely allows his emotions to blow the deal. He is a great actor. Yes, just like everyone else, he is more than one person based on the circumstances. Republicans worry that he does not have the experience to become President. It's quite laughable, as Barrack Obama had much less experience, and the Democrats got him elected a second time.

Furthermore, Mr. Trump is a serious threat to senators, congressmen, governors, and other elected officials. That's because he will not be influenced by all the special interest groups, race-baiters, and Wall Street, as Hillary Clinton has been over the past three decades. He also will not be swayed by the growing Muslim population who wish to transform American equalities, liberties, and law into a Sharia law. They are dedicated to eliminating other religions and beliefs. There is little doubt that hundreds of potential terrorists already operate within our borders. Donald Trump is right to take extra precautions with country with ties to Radical Islamic Terrorism.

What I see in Donald Trump is not based upon feelings of fanaticism. He is an admirable man; howbeit he is not someone I could be friends with. Nevertheless, the President of the United States does not take office to be everyone's friend. There is a difference between being friendly and being chummy. President Barrack Obama and Secretary Clinton want to be popular through decimation of the middle class. they want to be remembered by the minorities at the expense of the majority of America. Their policies and actions have created a welfare state that has attracted many illegal aliens into our country. Those who are fortunate to have jobs have to pay higher taxes to help those who stay on welfare, which pays more than finding employment.

Donald Trump wants everyone who is able to work to have a job. There is no bright future while living on government welfare. People want and deserve the opportunity to work for a better life for themselves and their family. The world has made many people in the United States feel ashamed to be Americans. We protect other nations; pay out trillions of dollars to help people in need. We send out thousands of troops and volunteers to help others in crises. Yet, there are many people in America who a homeless, destitute, and living in unsafe neighborhoods. People in nations we have helped mock us because out children score lower in STEM testing. An American Veteran often receives less benefits than an illegal alien. We permit immigrants to live contrary to our laws. Howbeit, if we were to travel to their native country, we would be jailed or killed for such behavior. America is going through an awakening unseen since WWII.

Fortunately, we are in a better situation than we were back then. The silent majority is vocal once more. We will soon be able to create an environment suitable for the

American family to thrive once again. We will no longer be silenced by the political correctness that allowed organizations, such as Black Lives Matter to prosper. Authority will return to law enforcement and our justice system. Crime rates will plummet, because people will be off the streets and working to Make America Great Again.

Donald Trump's Animosity toward NAFTA

On December 8, 1993, President Bill Clinton signed the North American Free Trade Agreement (NAFTA) into law. Since then, thousands of factories and businesses have closed and moved to Mexico or other foreign countries. Millions of jobs have been lost due to unfair competition with countries who want to sell to America, unrestricted. Yet, these same countries heap high tariffs upon the United States when we wish to sell to them. Companies and Corporations have layed-off millions of workers since then, and moved their operations to other countries where labor is cheap, business taxes are low, and they pay no import fees into the United States.

Donald Trump promises to renegotiate or eliminate NAFTA in order for the US to receive fair trade deals, protect intellectual property, and Make America Great Again. He has proven himself as a stellar negotiator, and has businesses worldwide. He, and his top executives, know how to get a good deal for Trump Organization and Donald Trump and his negotiators can do the same for the United States. In addition, Mr. Trump has promised to levy an import fee to

American corporations outside our country to make it less profitable for them to abandon their homeland.

Is America the Model for the Free World?

Many people view American citizens as self-righteous snobs who look down on citizens of other free countries as imitators of the United States. Speaking as a U.S. Citizen born and bred with ancestry extending six or more generations in the past, I have never felt superior to citizens of other countries. My opinion of other nations is that their country and people, for the most part, are wonderfully different in language, culture, and natural and cosmopolitan beauty. It actually disturbs me that some or our quirky lifestyles have taken root in other nations. Islamic extremism has taken root here, and now other nations feel they should condone it and other radical religious cultures.

In other words, the liberal ideals and thinking that has brought America to its knees have infected other nations, and continents. Now, stop to consider the impact that Donald J. Trump has made upon middle America. For the past year, the world has witnessed an awakening unlike any other era for decades. He came at a time when many Americans were about ready to toss in the towel. It took longer for his movement to affect opinions in Europe, as the Liberal press has desperately tried to downplay the Republican candidate while promoting the Democratic Candidate, Hillary Clinton.

Mostly-Polite Conversations

Presidents Who Build Glass Libraries

Saturday, May 07, 2016

I find is disgustingly deceitful, that President Barrack Hussein Obama would criticize Presidential Candidate Donald J. Trump for using election tactics reminiscent of his own in 2008. Of course, he would not publicly admit that he had used such tactics. Mr. Trump does not have the 'Privilege' of running as a minority, or woman. He cannot tout himself as the first 'African American' President, or the first 'Woman' president. Howbeit, he does have something no other President before him can claim. He is the first Presidential Candidate to run for office with no political or military experience.

Donald Trump's disadvantages is that he is a senior, rich, white guy. He is the 'poster child' of attacks from every minority in America. But, what is this? Millions upon millions of Americans have voted for this most despicable 'Reality Show' star. Could it be that the European-American billionaire philanthropist is not so bad after all?

Furthermore, why is President Obama so disrespectful toward Senator Bernie Sanders? Several times during his 'Presidential' speech, he mentioned Hillary Clinton as Secretary Clinton. Yet, not once did he include the term 'Senator' when mentioning Bernie Sanders. "Slap, slap, slap – Bernie Sanders," thinks our 'politically correct' President. President Obama's conduct over the last few weeks has been extremely lacking in Presidential protocol. "Islamic Terrorists Attack in Europe – "Go team go," shouts President Obama at a Cuban baseball game. More attacks in Europe – "Cha, cha, cha," whispers President Obama, while dancing the night away. That's right, Mr. President. The Presidency is not a reality show. It is real life, with real people.

When are you going to pay attention to your constituents, Mr. President? When are you going to finally admit that ISIS ends with an 'S' not an 'L', and that there is such a thing as a Radical Islamic Terrorist? Is it more Presidential to criticize a Presidential Candidate adored by hundreds of millions of American citizens. Keep building upon your 'legacy', Mr. President. Each brick you throw is one less reserved for the cornerstone of your 'Presidential'

library. Perhaps, you should build your library out of glass!
You're running out of bricks.

Misses the Mark

Dear Mr. Ip, I am one of the many educated
Republican supporters of Donald Trump. Therefore, I have
turned my attention to the Wall Street Journal with great
expectations of receiving informed and unbiased reporting of
the 2016 U.S. Presidential elections. Your article misses the
mark for much of the factual reporting I still hope to
encounter with the WSJ. It is true that the Washington Post,
and Facebook, are being used as unethical devices to sway the
public toward the left. This is why I am a fan of Fox News,
and the media they support. I enjoy the Journal reports, which
Fox News delivers.

I am unabashedly Republican. Most of America and I
have suffered and wept over the intolerable economic and
moral collapse of the United States due to the insane policies
of the Obama Administration, and Democratic Party. Like a
man gasping for his last breath, President Barrack Hussein
Obama wishes to destroy any remnant of sanity and moral
fiber he can find in the U.S.A. Nearly everything he had done
of late directly guarantees our destruction. Jobs are sorely

lacking; people worry about entering bathrooms; we are a joke to Russia, China, Iran, Iraq, Mexico. I could go on about where we are. However, I'd rather dream about 2017.

There are a few comments you made that actually makes sense. The following is not one of these. "As Mr. Trump understands well, voters care a lot less than wonks and journalists do about policy details." That is quite an inane statement Mr. Ip, because the chief reason Donald Trump is insanely popular is that he is a successful businessman, and not a politician. Your main argument is centered on what voters care about and not what they understand with regard to policy details. Trump supporters rave at the exciting and fresh initiatives that The Donald brings to the table. It has never been the President's job to give lessons on economics only to enlighten the public on a few basic terms and how it affects the American citizen. Wonks and journalists pretend to give sage advice concerning our nation's economy, yet often fall short of delivering impartial or comprehensive analysis of the same.

One thing you failed to mention is that Mr. Trump's prime initiative is getting America back to work. I am one of those citizens that ran out of unemployment benefits, and became a ward of the Obama Welfare State. Low paying jobs were available, yet they delivered fewer benefits than all the welfare freebees that had been heaped upon me. I retired early, as I refused to continue to suffer the embarrassment of 'entitlements' for my family and me.

We have more illegal immigrants today, because these people jump at the chance to get free education, housing, pay, and food stamps unavailable in Mexico, Central America, and South America. Furthermore, there is big money in selling drugs to the 'wealthy' Americans. It is also my opinion that children born to illegal immigrants should not be awarded citizenship until his or her parents reenter the United States legally and apply for citizenship. Awarding U.S. citizenship only to a baby is unfair to the family, and unfair to American taxpayers.

Welfare benefits and payments should never exceed the benefits of a job or career for those educated, trained, and capable of remaining in the workforce. Americans should always be rewarded for becoming bonafide taxpayers. More jobs means less welfare, and fewer entitlements. It also means more taxes can be collected to pay off our nation's soaring debt.

President Obama and the Democratic Party would rather have more people anxious to receive entitlements, which has driven our country deeper in debt. As you mentioned, Rep. Paul Ryan believes people really want to work and have control over his or her personal destiny. This is Donald Trump's message, as well. Make America Great Again by allowing citizens to receive and retain control over his or her own destiny.

I will look forward to reading any changes in attitude and wisdom concerning the elections, and topics that concern me as a U.S. Citizen. I am not through with my analysis of this column. I enjoy examining the facts and realistic projections of our economy. You can be sure that you have a reader who will help you keep your facts on the straight and narrow. By the way, Donald Trump does not prevaricate – he negotiates. It might behoove you to take some business negotiation classes. That's just a suggestion.

Political Discourse

Favored by All Kinds of Voters

Republican incumbents and candidates are under the allusion that supporting Donald Trump will cost him or her votes. However, party loyalty is valuable in any election. In this election, it is imperative. Once we consider that Senators are not restrained by an Electoral College, and understand that a Senator relies heavily upon the all-powerful voter to determine his or her fate, it is obvious they desperately need the immense voter base, which Donald Trump provides. My opinion is that Republican Senators, and all elected officials are underestimating the power and popularity of Donald Trump. The Donald overcame the 'rigged' Republican Primary system. He did it through a phenomenal voter turnout. If political candidates demonstrate disloyalty to *this* Republican Presidential Candidate, they run the risk of losing the confidence of millions of voters – Republicans, Independents, and Democrats. However, if they support Donald Trump, they will ride the Trump Train to victory, which is far better than receiving the support of so-called party loyalists.

Sticks and Stones Break Bones

I must admit that the Liberal media has done an excellent job of distorting the popularity and excellence of Donald J. Trump, while downplaying the corruption of Hillary, President Obama, and the Clinton Foundation. Most TV and internet networks demean any politically incorrect comment made by Donald Trump, while ignoring all the political corruption and failures of Hillary Clinton. Actions speak louder than words, just as sticks and stones break bones while words only bruise our egos.

Choosy Voters Choose Trump

Look how many states Donald Trump won in the primaries. It's the voter, this time, who will make or break the General Elections. If we had an incumbent Republican President this election, perhaps Donald may not have gotten past the guardians of the GOP. Of course, the incumbent would have had to be completing his or her second term, or have been a real rotten apple. As it was, Republican insiders were fighting tooth and nail to keep the election 'rigged' in favor of the Republican establishment.

Furthermore, we mustn't forget that Bernie Sanders supporters were hijacked by Democratic insiders as well. WikiLeaks continues to confirm how the DNC favored Hillary Clinton from the very beginning. Why are independent voters unable to recognize political corruption when it is laid so neatly at their feet? My opinion is that the opinion polls are all off-kilter. Personally, I believe Hillary and all her sad-sack Obama supporters will receive a grand comeuppance on November 8.

Simply Unpredictable

Pollsters have been unable to create a credible poll for a candidate who has never held a political office. This was proven repeatedly throughout the Primaries. Pollsters simply cannot forecast, with sufficient certainty, how voters will respond to a Clinton and Trump smack down. After Donald Trump quickly and efficiently eliminated some of the Republican Party's finest Presidential Candidates, I can't see Hillary Clinton doing much better.

Hillary is kept afloat by an extremely biased Liberal MSM, and one of the worst Presidents in US history, President Barack Hussein Obama. Howbeit, President Obama still maintains a winning popularity among his followers. Nevertheless, Hillary Clinton is losing her minority base due to low employment, low wages, and tens of millions of citizens on food stamps.

Furthermore, there is a large population of voters for Donald Trump who prefer to remain silent about his or her support for Donald Trump. As usual, the Democrats enjoy being caustic and physical regarding their favored candidate. Many voters have witnessed how Hillary and Sanders supporters have pummeled Trump supporters, removed

Trump campaign signs, and damaged cars and homes to threaten people who support Donald J. Trump.

Trump and the Establishment

Our federal government was established by people who were citizens of a new country, the United States of America. The people of the US created a government of representatives who were to represent their best interests when making decisions within our Judicial, Legislation, and Executive Branches of government. People who ruled according to his or her self-interests could be either voted out of office or impeached. Large groups of our population formed their own Political Party whose members supported political candidates who would make decisions in their favor.

However, as time went by, men and women of influence and wealth began to exert greater control over our government. People in power were influenced by bribes or favors from people who wanted, for example, throughways for railways, accommodations for building permits, etc. It was nearly impossible for anyone to run for a high political office without becoming a member of an established political party.

Today, we have two major political parties: the Democratic Party, and the Republican Party. There are several minor parties, as well, such as the Libertarian Party, the Green Party, et al. However, less than 10% of voters cast their ballots for these candidates. In 2000, Donald Trump had considered running on a minor party ticket, but decided against it. Mr. Trump learned that the race for President of the United States must be undertaken on a major party ticket. For years he supported the Democratic Party, and then he changed to the Republican Party after becoming disenchanted with the economic, military, and international trade policies of the Democrats. He felt compassion for the people of our nation who had made him so successful in business.

On June 16, 2015, Donald J. Trump announced his candidacy for President on the Republican Ticket. His slogan is, 'Make America Great Again'. This, of course, is offensive to the current presidential administration who support the Democratic Party. They believe America is already great under their rule. Donald Trump is a highly successful businessman, real estate mogul, author, and reality star of Celebrity Apprentice fame. However, he has never held an elected or appointed political office, nor served in the U.S. Armed Forces. On the other hand, he is well known and liked by many politicians. The Donald's fame and fortune helped him learn how the political system works, and brought him in contact with international leaders around the globe.

The non-politician Republican Candidate, Donald J. Trump, brought great excitement to a typically mundane Presidential Primary Election cycle. The media and most politicians did not take Mr. Trump's candidacy seriously. Most people believed the other 16 Republican Candidates would out-debate him on stage. What they did not consider was the Reality Television Star, author, and real estate tycoon's ability to negotiate with individuals and crowds. He soon became the center of attention at the debates with his unconventional and often outlandish responses and remarks. From the beginning, Donald Trump announced that one of the greatest problems we have in America today is believing we must be politically correct. He spoke his mind to fellow candidates and debate moderators alike.

Above all, it must be understood that the Presidential Election of 2016 is primarily between one electorate for the people and another for the government establishment. In nearly all past elections, and certainly those in modern times the contest has been between two political parties – the Democrats and the Republicans. The Democrats have taken a pro-government stance, and extol Liberalism in which they reason minority groups and special interests should take precedence over the majority of citizens. The Republicans believe in less government, and more freedom for people to take control of their own lives and businesses without government intervention. They believe in personal freedoms and majority rule.

Donald J. Trump changed all that when he became the Republican Nominee against the wishes of established members of the GOP. Then and since his nomination, he has had to compete against members of his own party who's major claim is that the down ballot race for the Senate has been weakened by Mr. Trump's nomination. Many people have also claimed that The Donald is no match for the political skills of an established Democrat, Hillary Clinton.
Mr. Trump was elected by the largest number of Primary votes in Republican history. He has become the 'People's Choice' for President of the United States.

The View

A lady Democrat from the city decided to spend a few days ruminating in the country. She stayed at a bed and breakfast that didn't have television, internet, cellular, or any connection to the outside world. She arrived late and went straight to bed. The next morning she awoke to an enchanting sound coming from outside her window. She opened the shades and was stunned by the natural beauty of the vista.

Dressing as quickly as she could, the city lady headed downstairs and observed the farmer's wife humming joyfully while exiting the back door with a basket in her hand. As she descended the staircase, she saw the farmer coming in the back door. She slyly mentioned to him, "You know, I really like The View." Rubbing his beard, and considering her sincerity, he responded, "Well, go ahead and have a look at it."

Skulking around outside, the city lady knew she was heading in the right direction as the angelic sound kept getting louder. The lovely sound became most intense as she came upon a door that had the words 'The View' above it. She was so thrilled when she opened the door, and heard the farmer's wife saying, "That's right, honey; You just give it up. Tomorrow's another day. Fry'em like bacon. That's what we'll do." The city lady looked around, and didn't see a television set anywhere. Yet, the sound was the same as she'd always remembered - a sweet music to her ears. "The farmer's wife must be hiding a wireless television in her basket," she thought.

Noticing she had been caught talking to herself, the farmer's wife muttered, "What's a matter, can't a lady have an opinion?" "Heaven's yes," responded the city lady. "I just love watching The View." "Well, okay," the farmer's wife responded, "Reach in that hole over there and grab me one." The city lady was a bit surprised, but reached in the hole and pulled out something that she had never seen before. "What is this," she stammered, "Is it some kind of communications device?"

The farmer's wife took the object, put it in her basket, and simply shook her head. Then, she confessed, "Sit down right here, city woman. Let me tell you how we country ladies enjoy ourselves." The city lady felt oddly comfortable sitting there listening to all the squabble coming from everywhere.

She continued to hear the wonderful banter of the ladies, and it made her feel like she was someone very special.

"Now, listen here, little lady. I'm a gonna tell you the same thing I told them there city slickers from the TV studio a few years back. When you hear the most disagreeable words you have ever heard in your lifetime, this is what you get. The farmer's wife pulled out of her basket, that strange object she had just seen and put it into the city lady's hand. Only, this one was cracked. You see, this here is an egg; them there are chickens, and you're sittin' in one of the most heavenly places in life, a chicken coop. Them lady producers loved 'The View' so much, they made one of their own and they ain't never been back.

The city lady held the cracked egg in her hand, and gazed at the tiny feathers floating in the air – illuminated by sunlight shining through the loose shingles. She named one of the hens Whoopi, as she made the most reprehensible noise. "I think I'll stay a little longer," she whispered to herself. The clucking, the squawking, the sounds made no sense, yet they comforted her, and made her feel at home.

Another enchanting tale, by Jeffrey L Kelley

Dinosaurs no More

I remember, during the Midterm Elections of 2014, the Democrats claimed that Republicans were going the way of the dinosaur. They were all on cloud 9 after President Obama was reelected in 2012. Then, the hammer came down and the Republican Party overwhelmed the Democrats by landslide victories in both the House of Representatives and the Senate. The Democratic Party took a lot of heat for their baseless chiding of Republicans, yet they still insist that the Republican Party is unpopular. They believe conservatism is outdated and will soon disappear as a major political party. If either major party would fail without a replacement, it may prove to be a problem for America. America thrives on competition, good or bad.

This time around, we have Donald J. Trump as our Republican Nominee. He was considered good entertainment in the beginning, and then seasoned politicians began to fall by the wayside. The Democratic Party was laughing at how upset the Republican establishment was getting, as Donald Trump was winning state after state in the Republican Primary Elections. Nevertheless, now the laughter is coming from the people and it's time for the Liberals to deal with Donald

Trump. The Democrats must understand that they were the ones, more precisely the Obama Administration, who encouraged Mr. Trump to run for office. The Democrats actually believed they were the future of modern politics. Today, with a renewed zeal for nationalism due to global acts of terrorism, the passing of Brexit, and the loss of millions of jobs for industries moving out of America, the Democratic Party may be destined for Jurassic Park.

Trump-Charting through Political Controversy

There are so many facets to the story of the Donald J. Trump Presidential Candidacy. We look here and there seeking to fathom the complexity of his persona and often come up empty handed as he, once again, changes the political narrative. Yet, there are a few guidelines we can follow to help us understand and maybe even prognosticate where and how The Donald will strike next. The reader must understand that in nearly every circumstance Mr. Trump has a plan to turn any controversy into a point in the winner's column. Many people believe he shoots from the hip. Howbeit, how lucky can one be with a lack of political correctness? The Donald seems to emit an impermeable force field when it comes to attacks from the Left, and has perfected a superglue counterpunch to send his oppressors reeling for days from political shock.

I have made it my mission to create some type of method to reflect Donald Trump's decision-making process. Flow charts are not as popular as they once were. However, when I retired from the military, equipment repair manuals used a troubleshooting chart that guided a technician to find a fault in the electronic or mechanical system of each unit. I'm going to use a current topic of discussion, such as Trump

University, to help me pinpoint various tactics used by Donald Trump to overcome a controversy, which has drawn a hefty amount of media attention.

It never fails to amaze me how the news media leaves out pertinent details from the stories they broadcast or publish. The Liberal media often vilifies Donald Trump whatever he does or says. They twist the story into a fashion that aides their pet candidate, Hillary Clinton. Simply watch CNN, and you will find that anything negative about Hillary Clinton is blacked out of daily news coverage. That isn't to say that everything reporters say about Donald Trump on CNN is always inaccurate. Howbeit, even Republican representatives who are supposed to support Donald Trump make comments and hasty decisions over media hype. Often, they are afraid of catching flak from their own constituency, or that down ballot candidates will get negative press as well.

Redeeming American Ethics and Values

Lately, it's been difficult to find a decent article about Donald Trump. Now that he has more than enough votes to be the Republican Nominee, reporters have shifted to the Clinton/Sanders competition. It's probably best for Mr. Trump to see how badly Bernie stomps on Hillary. Hillary has been carried aloft by her superdelegates since the beginning of the Primaries. She has been coroneted Queen of the DNC before any voter threw the first lever.

Hillary's reign, we pray, is almost over. Bernie has great momentum. If Hillary loses or barely wins California, it will mean a few more nails in her coffin. If Hillary is indicted by the FBI, it's time to call the undertaker. If Hillary Clinton were to be elected, she would continue the Barrack Obama agenda, drive America deeper in debt, allow our enemies to take new territory, and frustrate our military and our friends.

Until the General Election contest officially begins, I will have to pray that people carefully examine what the Democratic Party has done to our beloved country. If we open our borders like they did in Europe, we can surely expect the same chaos they are experiencing. If we secure our borders, and keep Islamic Terrorists and illegal immigrants at bay, we can enjoy the peace and prosperity of a nation dedicated to protecting its citizens. We must do all we can to stop the influx of people who have no love for America's laws, and morality.

No matter the impetus of the British movement to exit the Liberal European Union, I can't help but believe that the Donald Trump movement of the United States has had a positive effect on patriots everywhere. I believe that America's founding fathers had it right when they said America was created by the people and for the people. We believe the government works for us, and not the other way around. When sovereign states lose their rights to bear arms, their religious freedom, and citizenship based upon legal and moral principles, something is mightily wrong. The Trump movement now has a foreign ally in our quest to return America to greatness. We should now consider a phrase such as Make America and Britain Great Again.

Why Me?

"What happened?" I said, as I sat up in my bed again shaking off the cobwebs and drooling for my morning cup of coffee. I remember the last time I felt this bewildered. It was 2012, and Mitt Romney had just lost the Presidential Election to President Barrack Obama. I was severely confused. How could half of America, and a bunch of confused Electoral College Delegates have voted a phenomenally incompetent president back into office? But, wait a minute. I looked at the calendar. It's only May, and November is six months away. We still have a chance, I think.

What was my last coherent thought? Oh, yeah, Donald Trump will soon be the official Republican Nominee for President. It still made me uneasy. It isn't t that I don't believe in Donald Trump. I have every faith in his abilities and judgement. I also know that he is wildly popular, and his followers are growing by the thousands every day. The problem is that our current leadership in the GOP just won't let go.

Imagine standing on the battlefield about to face the enemy. Our general raises his sword about to call the charge.

He looks to his left and to his right and discovers something quite odd. All of his officers have abandoned their posts. Yet, further back are millions of troops who are counting on his leadership, and his leadership alone. What should he do? Without hesitation, he calls his top sergeants and promotes them all to officers. The army is now ready. The general thinks to himself, "Maybe, it's better this way." Then, his horse raises itself on its two hind legs General Trump bellows, "Charge!"

This is how I feel about the Republican Party right now. Donald J. Trump has already made history as the highest Presidential Primary vote-getter in our nation's history. Still, Paul Ryan and many other Republican senators, congressmen, governors, et. al. are wasting this historic opportunity by holding back his or her endorsements. It made me think about Romney's election in 2012. Almost four years ago, our leaders failed our nominee. I saw and felt the criticism of our elected officials slowly shrink away from their elected posts.

Today, all I can ask myself is, "Why me?" Why should I invest my emotions and soul in a campaign that already seems on the brink of disaster? At the end of the Presidential Elections of 2012, I had been living in Peru for nearly a year.

I hadn't even secured a voter's registration in my home state of Michigan before leaving the United States, as I had just relocated there from Indiana before leaving for Peru. I hold myself responsible for not casting my vote for my favored representatives back then. I now have to finish what I started back then. Monday morning, I'm going to check on my voter's registration and ensure it is current. Then, I will request mail-in election forms when they become available. It takes about ten days for mail to reach a U.S. destination on the best of days. I will have to work faster as Christmas mail, even in October, causes a further delay.

Nevertheless, I will not let distance or circumstances prevent my vote from being cast this time around. So, this is me asking the question many Americans ask around voting time, "Why me?" I am not alone in feeling that all the hope and zeal I have held for my personal candidate might again be squashed by a heartless government that has served its donors more than its people. "Why me," is asked by many voters across the United States no matter the political affiliation.

After all, if anyone took to heart what happened to the popular vote in the Electoral College in 2012 and especially within the Democratic and Republican Parties during the

Primaries, they now feel powerless to effect change. Look at the condition of our country today. Nearly eight years of President Obama and the Democratic Party has brought our country to its knees.

Here is the hope I have this election cycle. Mr. Donald J. Trump entered the race as a private citizen. He has never held an elected office. He holds no favors to special interest groups, businesses, or governments. He has paid for his own campaign to date. Many opponents have pointed to his failed business ventures, yet he is a billionaire – with a 'b'. He has been married three times, but his children love him and his ex-wives hold him in high regard.

Beyond all that, to say he knows little about politics is erroneous. Nobody becomes successful in business and real estate without rubbing elbows and greasing palms. Mr. Trump has also traveled the world, and knows how Japan, China, Germany, and other nations tick. Finally, Donald Trump overcame the 'rigged' party system to become, not the Party favorite, but the voice of the people. He has gained votes from Republicans, Democrats, and Independents. If ever there was an opportunity for change in the United States ever since the election of Abraham Lincoln, it is found in Donald J. Trump.

Trumps Contract with America

- 5 year ban on representatives becoming lobbyists
- Lifetime ban on White House officials lobbying
- Ban on foreign lobbyists contributing to American elections

Trump's 100 Day Action Plan

- Constitutional Amendment to impose term limits on all members of Congress
- For every new Congressional Regulation, two existing regulations must be eliminated.
- We will cancel all federal funding of 'Sanctuary Cities.'
- We will begin removing 2 million criminal illegal immigrants from the country.
  - These are drug dealers, gang heads, gang members, killers
- We are going to suspend immigration from terror-prone regions where vetting cannot safely occur.
- Fully repeal Obamacare and replace it with health savings accounts

Our Story

Our story has no veritable beginning. And, hopefully, we have no final resolution. Humans, throughout the ages, have relied on leaders to keep families, clans, and civilizations safe from the elements and marauding factions who wish to steal or destroy centuries of human wisdom and progress. It is ignorance, which is our greatest foe. Today, the military might of the United States of America is the only thing that separates the entrepreneurship of a free people from the domination of foreign powers. Understand that dictators and tyrants only need people to make them more powerful and wealthy.

America is on the precipice of greatness, or oblivion. Our government has turned its back upon the people who lent them their power. America was built upon "We the people ..." and we can rescind our power when our elected officials no longer represent us and endanger our "inalienable rights of life, liberty, and the pursuit of happiness."

During the past seven and one-half years, we have seen a great erosion of our three-tiered system of government. We have seen our Legislative Branch, the Senate and House of Representatives deadlocked and unable to create the laws we need for effective governance. The Judicial Branch of government has been usurping the authority of the Legislative Branch by making laws of their own, and overruling State laws that represent the will of the people. The Executive Branch of Government, the Presidency, prefers executive orders or veto powers over the majority vote of the House and Senate. This, by itself, is more representative of tyranny than of the will of the people.

All of these aforementioned can and will be debated by so-called experts of the Constitution. However, nobody in the Judicial, Legislative, or Executive Branches of Government can refuse the will of the people. Finally, this is where my story begins about the greatest representative of 'We the People...' since the founder of the Republican Party, Abraham Lincoln. We find this representative in Republican Candidate for President of the United States, Donald J. Trump. The free-thinking citizens of the United States have chosen a leader who will represent them, and Make America Great Again.

It was a difficult struggle for Donald Trump to overcome the 'rigged system' of the Republican National Convention (RNC). What people, including me, failed to understand was that both the Democratic and Republican Parties are organizations, which are designed to protect the people and policies of the organization. In other words, they operate under the premise that their business is more important than the personal welfare of their constituents.

If the Republican Party had believed Donald Trump had a remote possibility of winning, they would have denied him membership through false accusations of party disloyalty or some other contrived charge. Fortunately, the Grand Old Party (GOP) ignored the popularity of candidate, just as they consistently ignore the will of the people in day to day politics. This time, their nefarious practice worked to the advantage of the citizens of the United States.

Modern America and the Constitution of the United States of America

The Republican Party has changed over the years, and so has America's Constitution. Howbeit, much of the Constitution followed by our forefather's is adhered to in modern America. We have freedom of speech, freedom of assembly, right to bear arms, et al. Yet, the United States has changed over the years. For example, we have more states. Each states provide a certain flavor to our heritage, and to our way of life. Colonial America were separated by religion, and differing commerce, and educational systems. Our Constitution provides for the right of states to decide on laws not provided for in our Constitution. As time passed, the Constitution changed and, at times, superceded discriminatory practices voted into law by each state. A number of acts allowed for women to vote, and all U.S. Citizens upon reaching the legal age to vote were (eventually) given the power to do so.

Today, the Legislative Branch of Government continues to create laws, which are then carried out by the Executive Branch. The Judicial Branch only intervenes if there is a dispute over the interpretation of the law. To be sure, when no federal laws exist, each state has the right to make its own laws.

The President of the United States cannot change laws created by Congress. He or she cannot write executive orders to circumvent laws. Unfortunately, our three-tiered government has been eroded by elected officials who want to promote special interest groups over the population majority. For years, government contracts to foreign and domestic entities have been bought and sold by corrupt politicians. This practice is so deeply entrenched in government, that the last two major political parties, Democrats and Republicans, had made it nearly impossible for an outsider to break the unfair and unpopular practices of our elected representatives.

Today, elections are more popularity contests than an honest effort to effect change in our government, especially within our nation's capital. It's become common practice for any politician to make promises he or she knows cannot be kept. I used to believe that the reason for this error was that they were more than a bit naïve as to the political machine they were about to face. On the other hand, what about the incumbents. They are already in office and know what they can or cannot accomplish. Their competition makes absurd promises and they, in turn, attempt to make promises beyond their capabilities.

What, then, are we to do with politicians who are 'locked-in' to agreements with organizations who fund their election campaigns? This has been the way of elections for decades. How can someone, who honestly wants to change 'business as usual' in Washington? Modern elections for the Presidency now cost hundreds of millions of dollars. Presidential candidates requires a huge donor base to fund his or her campaign. The easiest thing to do is gain massive contributions from rich Americans, and superfunds. In the end, these contributions are repaid by favors from the candidate when he or she takes office.

I mentioned earlier that politics has become a game of popularity. If one can gain the respect and admiration of millions of Americans, he or she may have a chance at becoming President of the United States. I say 'a chance' as popularity by the American public has been a second objective of politicians until this election. The Electoral College takes precedence over the popular vote. Moreover, who makes up the Electoral College? People who were put in place by elected officials, of course.

In the Presidential Primaries, each state elects delegates to represent the 'people' of the state. Once again, many of these delegates can be 'persuaded' to vote for the Party's choice. Of course, the political party denies any favoritism showered upon its favored candidate. Howbeit, it becomes quite obvious to the American public who the political party really wants in office.

Funding One's Own Political Campaign

In my last article, Modern America and the Constitution of the United States of America, I purposely avoided naming names of our current Presidential Candidates. I did so in order to show how Presidential elections are run, without cluttering the landscape with political bias of parties and candidates. Any candidate for President, if he or she has any chance to win an election, must understand that the cost of such a venture is huge, complex, and beset by political pitfalls. For the average American, and even multi-millionaires, funding one's own political campaign is out of the question. Only the richest of the rich has the money for such an endeavor.

Then, there is Donald J. Trump, who was the first Presidential Candidate in modern history to fund his own Presidential Primary, and is the principal contributor to his General election campaign. His announcement to run for President on June 16, 2015 has been revisited numerous times throughout his campaign. The Donald's campaign slogan, Make America Great Again, was first announced that day and has become a rallying cry for tens of millions of people. The news media and political pundits were having a field day discussing Mr. Trump's entrance into politics. It all seemed like just such fun, until the Republican Candidate Debates, and Primary Elections began.

What was most unusual about his announcement was that he said he would fund his own political campaign. It is this announcement, I believe, that caused many staunch establishment Republicans to wring their hands. It had to be a concern. Special interest groups, large corporations, and foreign governments for the first time they could remember would be out of business with this guy. However, not to worry, there were 17 other candidates who were sure to tromp on Trump. Soon, his announcement would just be a laughable memory. Or, so they thought.

"We the People ..."

Preamble to the U.S. Constitution

"We the People of the United States, in Order to form a more perfect Union, establish Justice, insure domestic Tranquility, provide for the common defense, promote the general Welfare, and secure the Blessings of Liberty to ourselves and our Posterity, do ordain and establish this Constitution for the United States of America"

The White House is neither the retirement home nor hospice imagined by Hillary Rodham Clinton. It is the home of our First Family a place of family values, ethics, and abundant patriotism. We are all aware how President Bill Clinton ran the Oval Office as his personal harem. President Clinton was the second US President to be successfully impeached by the House of Representatives, due to his lies concerning his sexual affair with a personal intern. Meanwhile, Hillary Rodham Clinton as First Lady exercised her misandrist tendencies to use the U.S. Secret Service as 'whipping boys' and treated Bill's abused women as desirous hussies who dared to accuse her husband of improper advances. This is the Clinton legacy they wish we would forget.

On November 8, 2016, we the voters of the United States will cast our ballot for a President who will dominate our Executive Branch of Government for the next four years. Will we decide to vote for Hillary Clinton's higher taxes, higher debt, fewer jobs, and greater crime and terror within our porous borders? On the other hand, will we vote for Donald Trump who champions greater control of our boarders, carefully vetted legal immigration, lower taxes, more jobs, higher wages, and an economy dedicated to America first? Your vote counts! Donald J. Trump succeeded against the rigged RNC only because 'We the people' stood up to be counted.

"... this nation, under God, shall have a new birth of freedom -- and that government of the people, by the people, for the people, shall not perish from the earth."
Abraham Lincoln November 19, 1863 (Bliss copy of Gettysburg Address)

Shall we allow HRC to continue her 'pay to play' activities within the highest office of the land? Will we give her the opportunities to open our borders to invite higher numbers of terrorists, rapists, and murderers? How will we defend ourselves when she pries our guns from our hands by eliminating our precious Second Amendment 'right to bear arms'? If anyone doubts the immense power that the Clinton Foundation exerts over the press and MSM, he or she will surely awaken to a government-controlled press once HRC takes office.

Do not be swayed by the relentless lies coming from the mouth of Hillary Clinton. One only has to listen to her testimony before the FBI and Congress to realize she is incapable of rendering the truth to a naïve public, and obsequious press. From one side of her mouth she preaches women's rights, and from the other side she praises Saudi Arabia, a nation that enslaves women, for their generous contributions to the Clinton Foundation. Howbeit, don't worry about being heard by 'Her Highness'. Save a few hundred thousand dollars and she may lend you a few minutes of her time.

Stand now! Stand for Donald Trump and Mike Pence in 2016. Don't wake up on November 9 to find a mosque on every corner, a For Sale sign in your front yard. Say no to a government controlled by foreign powers and the Washington elite. Say yes to the America our forefathers envisioned when they crafted the Constitution of the United States of America. When you vote Trump/Pence, you vote 'We, the People'.

A Latecomer to the World of Have

How many times have I begun a page only knowing the subject of which I was to write, but not knowing what to write about it, him, or her? This is where I am, yet again. As you know, I am writing about someone who will hold the lives of all Americans in his hands. We have grown accustomed to a government that, on the surface, appears to represent the citizens of this great nation, the United States of America. However, we have known for a long time that beneath that thin veneer of campaign promises and vain posturing of presidential candidates is an illusion designed to pacify middle America into believing we have a future beyond our mundane daily toils and weekend parties. Decade after decade we labored until the day arrived when we could finally rest from our professions and enjoy the fruits of our labor. Yet, when that day arrived we discovered retirement and savings were not enough to pay for all the medicines, doctors, and daily expenses that we had managed to pay while working.

Many retirees, and indeed many healthy young men and women struggle to put food on the table, clothes on our backs, and a roof over our heads. Moreover, within walking distance of our humble abodes are stores, restaurants, and health facilities, which contain all the necessities we struggle to achieve. Are they there to inspire us to work harder while we have the vitality to bring home a paycheck, or as a reminder of some paradise we may never truly visit?

Then there are the people who work as salespeople, maintenance workers, and security guards who work in and around malls and shopping centers where they can only hope to purchase a few items of low value with whatever remains from his or her paltry paycheck. All these people and millions more labor for a better life that often seems just out of reach. Is it any wonder that people decide to work two or more jobs, if they don't otherwise decide that crime may be his or her best avenue of escape?

I used to be one of the working class with little education beyond high school. I've served my country in the military, labored in factories, department stores, and even had a couple of small businesses. Later in life, I finally graduated from college and hoped to obtain a job that provided me with a salary worthy of my education and experience. It was a bad time to begin a new profession for two reasons. The economy was depressed, and I was quickly nearing retirement. Still, I felt I had a lot to offer as a teacher. After all, I knew what it was like for a student with little education to land a good job. It was my hope to spend the next ten to twenty years imparting my life experiences upon the starry-eyed youth whose early decisions would make or break them.

Finding little opportunity in the United States, I traveled to Peru where there was much need to learn English as a Foreign Language. The little money I earned teaching and some early retirement money has gone much further here. Now that I am receiving every possible bread crumb from Social Security, a military pension, and other income, I see some hope in returning to the United States. Still, I cannot return to the dismal economy I left behind.

It is my hope that Donald Trump will impart his great economic and business sense upon our nation. Of all the past Presidents for whom I have voted, he seems to have to right ideas to return our great nation to its former glory. Make America Great Again. It has a glorious ring to it. Please understand that my family is one of those families who have members born outside the United States. We are paying the price for my wife and stepson to become legal citizens of the United States. The faulty policies of Hillary Clinton and

Barack Obama to grant clemency to all those who arrived in America illegally really make us angry, and we are not alone.

My hope is that Donald Trump will make it easier for law-abiding people from other nations to receive citizenship. It is absolutely unfair, and unlawful to reward criminals for his or her illegal actions. They must pay their fines, fees, taxes, and time-in-line as those of us who desire to do what is good and right for our country. Believe it or not, it is more difficult to become a citizen of Peru, as its citizens have to deal with a government bureaucracy that looks for any way to tax or fine anyone seeking to rise above his or her social status, or make an honest income.

President of the United States

Our U.S. Constitution assures us that any decent law-abiding citizen of the right age could become President of the United States. These are the requirements: male or female, natural born citizen, 35 years or older. That's all there is to it. However, if you want a chance at winning, there is that little matter of getting 100,000 signatures from voters of *each* state, and gathering a few hundred million dollars to pay for advertising, traveling across the United States, an election staff, et. al.

Hey, anyone can run as an independent, right. Well, that isn't right. Your best chance is to run as either a Democrat or Republican, apply to their campaign committee, and receive their approval to run. The reason for this is that they provide tremendous resources and support for your presidential campaign, if you meet their expectations. Most importantly, you must publicize a political platform that agrees with the party who supports you. Now, what if you have never run for office, but are an internationally known celebrity, and a billionaire to boot? You just might have a better chance than other people of much lesser reputation and currency.

A Donald Trump/Mike Pence Administration

I am full of hope as I consider the glorious opportunities all Americans will share with a Donald Trump Presidency. We have never completely recovered from the Great Recession we experienced in 2009. What's more, the United States has accumulated another ten trillion dollars in debt. The Obama Presidency has turned our nation into a welfare state, drawing millions of illegal immigrants (tens of thousands under Obama's approval) to drain our country's resources. Even our honored Veterans do not receive the benefits heaped upon the foreigners who have invaded our sovereign nation. Donald Trump and Mike Pence have the combined expertise to Make America Great Again.

A Hillary Clinton/Tim Kaine Administration

There are millions of Americans who believe a female duplicate of President Obama would be a good thing for our beleaguered homeland. If Hillary Clinton were to become President of the United States, it would be a coup d'état or death blow to our struggling citizens. Are people blind to America's loss of jobs, and increased poverty? Do we need another leader who is soft on crime, terrorists, and riots in our streets? Recent events have proven that Hillary Clinton is untrustworthy, a liar, and a criminal. She is ready to sell America to the highest bidder, and place our military arsenal in mothballs. Now, at a time when we need a true leader, should voters consider electing a leader based on her sex, rather than her record of success?

Learning from Past Mistakes

I invite every U.S. Citizen who is able to vote to consider what America will look like in four to eight years if another Liberal occupies the White House. Donald J. Trump is a proven businessman who can negotiate with world leaders and corporations. He has proven his prowess in several nations, and has nothing to gain by leaving his wealth in a living trust in order to pay America back for all his worldly gains.

His altruism can be compared to Andrew Carnegie, who sometimes was considered a self-serving debutant as he built his lucrative steel industry. He was blamed for the deaths of 10 people during the Homestead Strike of 1892. Yet, throughout most of his life he donated greatly to charities. He is known today as the greatest benefactor to libraries and educational institutions across the United States. Donald J. Trump, even during his costly campaign for president, has donated millions to charities, as well. Nevertheless, like Andrew Carnegie, he is often remembered for his failures rather than his successes.

The Peruvian Perspective

I have often conversed with Gabriela's Aunt Lucy about the Presidential Elections in the United States. She has been kind to entertain my verbal ramblings. We have conversed often and she, I believe, has found it somewhat entertaining. One day, I spoke with Juan Celi Diaz, Gabriela's brother, amidst some guests that has gathered early for a birthday party. It was the first time that I had heard an emotional opinion in Peru about who the next U.S. President would be. His brother, Pepe, married a woman in the United States and he has been a citizen for some time now. Juan was concerned about his brother if Donald Trump should become the next President of the United States. The only American news station we can get here in Peru is CNN International in Spanish and in English. Because CNN is pro-Hillary, many Peruvians who have relatives in the United States are afraid they will be sent back to Peru. I informed Juan that Pepe is a U.S. Citizen and not an illegal immigrant.

I explained to Juan, and other friends and relatives that illegal immigration, and refugees from Syria and other nations who have run from ISIS in the middle-east have caused many economic, and crime problems in the United States. Donald

Trump wants to rid our nation of criminals who are in the US illegally, secure our borders, and institute a better program of ensuring legal citizenry. I informed my small audience that Hillary Clinton would cause more problems for legal citizens across the United States. Our country would experience great economic hardships, and personal security of all residents would be at greater risk.

Those who wish to remain in the United States should do everything they can to become legal citizens. That may become a serious hardship to some, yet becoming a US Citizen would offer them greater benefits, and peace of mind. When my mother-in-law, Milena, applied for a Visa to visit Pepe in the US, I helped her with the paperwork. She passed with flying colors, and was able to visit him for a few months. I admit that I miss all the luxuries my homeland has to offer, and was happy that Milena learned a little bit about the life that two of my boys, and I left behind.

I am very angry with CNN for their biased international broadcasts of the Presidential Election. They do a great disservice to our citizens living abroad. As a retired US Veteran Ex-Patriot, it grieves me to have to tell my Peruvian family and friends that the Liberal news media has been spreading political propaganda, a term I had only applied to Communists and dictators of other countries in the past. This is what we have had to deal with over the past eight years. The truth is quickly squelched by news organizations controlled by companies who support the Democratic Party. Hollywood, and special interest groups wish our middle-class citizens to remain under their immoral control. When our citizenry allows itself to become dependent upon a government to provide for their needs, we are no longer free, but subjects of a ruling upper class.

About the Author

After living most of my life in the United States, yet visiting other countries while serving in the military, and nearly retired, my fiancé and I decided it would be more feasible and lucrative for my two American boys and I to move to Peru. Gabriela, Gabriel, and I met on the internet and after a few months of email and video correspondence, I traveled to Chiclayo, Peru to spend time with my future bride and stepson and meet Gaby's mother, sister, and extended family. I visited for a couple months, left for the United States and then returned two months later with Charlie and Tommy. Ever since then we can be seen as a curiosity on the streets of Chiclayo. My two American boys speak better Castilian than I do, and my Peruvian son is speaking better English than nearly all of his classmates.

Besides a multitude of courses in military communications, I received a Latin American Spanish Language Certificate from the prestigious Defense Language Institute, in the Presidio of Monterey, California. My formal education includes a B.S. in Business Organization with postgraduate studies in Elementary Education from Bethel College, Mishawaka, Indiana. I also received an M.A. Ed in

Adult Education and Training from Argosy University, Phoenix, Arizona. Furthermore, I have completed over a year of studies toward an Ed.D with emphasis in ESL with Northcentral University, of Phoenix, Arizona. I taught English at a local English Institute, Instituto Cultural Peruano Norte Americano (ICPNA), here in Chiclayo, Peru for over a year before teaching Business English courses for Top Class English, in addition to tutoring small groups and one-on-one lessons at my private residence.

One reason why I moved to Peru was the lack of opportunity for teaching as an older adult within the United States. While living here in Peru, I found that lack of citizenship has restricted me from teaching at public and private educational institutions. On the other hand, private teaching is in high demand in Peru, especially when the teacher is from the United States or another English-speaking country.

Why Donald Trump?

Donald Trump was not my first pick this election. I was still hung-up on Mitt Romney, believing he should have been elected President in 2012. I was not a fan of the TV series, Celebrity Apprentice, and 'The Donald' did not seem like someone I could relate to. However, as Mitt Romney seemed to have been left by the wayside by the GOP, I reluctantly began to follow Donald Trump. None of the other Republican Candidates really impressed me, and Hillary Clinton with her skirt-chasing husband were never under consideration. After all, she was no better than President Obama in failed economic policies and practices.

It wasn't long before Donald J. Trump began to grow on me. I researched his past, and I was truly impressed with how he helped revive New York City, during 1970's and 80's. I still can't believe how someone so incredibly wealthy would want to surrender his comfortable lifestyle to become President of the United States. It must be in his blood. His love for the ordinary man and woman really inspires me.

So, here I am writing about someone who has become an inspiration to me and many other Americans who really want to do something with his or her life. I have learned something about our news media today, as well. Few can be trusted to present unbiased opinions and facts about our Republican Nominee, Donald J. Trump. I watch Fox News to get most of my daily news, and watch CNN to see if the network will deliver some small morsel of unbiased reporting. I also read and watch the Wall Street Journal, and research books and biographies off the internet.

The Kelley's of Peru

Charles, Gabriela, Jeff, Thomas, & Gabriel

Jeffrey & Gabriela Celi Diaz de Kelley

Married in Peru, October 25, 2013